PRESENCE, DISTILLED

Dear Heather,

It is my hope some parts (or many) of this book resonate with you. Thank you for being present and vulnerable with me.

I am grateful.

Cate

Library of Congress Control Number: 2022922681
ISBN 979-8-218-11926-3
EPUB ISBN 979-8-218-11927-0
First edition, 2022
PCIP data upon request

This activity is made possible by the voters of Minnesota through a grant from the Southeastern Minnesota Arts Council thanks to a legislative appropriation from the arts and cultural heritage fund.

For my many mentors, especially Jim Hancock,
I take you with me everywhere:
"Onwards and Upwards."

Contents

Prologue

My first book, *Leadership, Distilled* is something I feel "wrote me." While it was years in the making—the stories, experiences, and haiku all came together in the wake of 2020—that strange year where lockdown unlocked a torrent of unlearning. When asked who my target audience was, I had difficulty nailing that answer down.

This book is different. I know precisely who this book is for: It's for anyone, at any age or juncture of life, who craves, as the French say, *je ne sais quoi*—that certain something that sets you apart from the rest of the crowd. Translated to English, it means a quality one cannot easily describe.[1] In essence, it means presence.

What sort of street credit do I have? For over three decades, I have been a professional performing artist (who, as you will see, has a great love of haiku poetry, Shakespeare, and storytelling). I spent many years receiving training on stage presence. I was taught:

All the world's a stage...[2]

For the past twenty years, I have been translating that training and experience onto one of the most significant stages in the world: Business. There, I help people cultivate their leadership presence.

Over time I began distilling my work into five points— **Breath, Posture, Gesture, Content,** and **Mindset.**

When developed and attended to, these five areas can imbue us with stellar presence. Honing each of these skills will make that elusive thing—that we still can't necessarily name— into something we can harness, then become.

I aim to help you cultivate a deepened awareness of these building blocks *and* give you practical guidance in unleashing your unique personal brand of presence.

Chapter 1

On Learning

Learning takes Patience
Practice then Practice Again
Perception is Key

As we begin this journey of distilling presence down to its core components, I find it helpful to take a moment to consider the learning process.

When I work with clients, whether in a group setting or one-on-one, one of my first questions is:

How do you learn best?

Take a moment to sit with that question. Consider when and how a lesson is most impactful.

Do you learn by watching and imitating others?
Do you like to be in a group setting, or do you want to sequester and learn on your own in your own time?
Do you learn by doing, with the act of physical repetition?

Do you need time and space to process? Do you feel
compelled to take notes and write things down—
even if you never return to those notes again?
Are you more impacted by listening and hearing?
Or, since you picked this book up, I will follow a hunch
and ask if you learn by reading?

I ask these questions because I don't know that we empower learners often enough to consider their processes. By asking such questions, we open the door to a sense of wonder, which is critical to learning.

When a client says to me, "I've never thought about that before," I know we are getting somewhere. An opening is created. The state of wonder is where the magic begins.

If that got a little too woo-woo for you, bear with me... I believe magic is critical to the learning process. When I say magic, I mean the ability to suspend your disbelief and step into the realm of imagining and experiencing things you aren't necessarily comfortable with—a willingness to flail, flop, then fly.

Here is another way to think of it in the journey of discovering presence:

It is required you do awaken your Faith.

That line is taken from *The Winter's Tale*.[3] It is one of my favorite plays by Shakespeare because it is all about learning, forgiveness, and awakening oneself to the possibilities that life holds in store, regardless of your age.

Presence requires us to awaken and practice having faith in ourselves. Who we are. How culture, our beliefs, our physical circumstances, and our choices shape us. Before going any further, take a few moments and reflect upon your learning style. Reflect upon others' styles too. Take this space provided here, and take some notes on it. See what comes up for you.

I'd also like you to consider the ideal environment in which you learn. (Is it in person or virtual? Do you prefer working in small groups, large groups, or one-on-one? Or describe another setting that suits you.)

What is it about those specific environments that help you absorb the material and excel?

Lastly, do you have faith in your ability to learn new things? What does it look like to you to discover and take ownership of your brand of Presence? Think back to how your presence has shifted over the years. What is it you want to offer the world next?

Now that you have taken the time to answer these questions, please set aside all that you know about yourself and try something new.

A contradiction? Yes. Most certainly. But learning is funny—it calls for paradox, or at least permitting yourself the time and space to live in and experience the unknown for a while. As you read this book, be sure to allow space for contradictions and experimentation.

Awareness of your biases and willingness to set those aside so that something new can occur creates an ideal state to begin the learning process. In Zen teachings, it is called "Beginner's Mind."[4]

Additionally, if you find yourself in a learning situation where you may be in the spotlight and feeling pressure, can you speak up about what may not be jibing for you? If you can—it can help your coach immensely!

It's important to remember a coach, facilitator, or teacher can only create so much psychological safety in a room, especially if working together with a large group. While we coaches may be keen observers, we are not mind readers. You, as a learner, *always* have the right to speak up, ask questions, and ask to take breaks—or leave all together. So take conscious note of your feelings as you enter the learning process. Listen to your intuition.

An important question to ask yourself when feeling uncomfortable in the learning process is, "What's mine, and what's yours?"

Ask yourself: are you feeling a certain discomfort because you are embarrassed you don't know this yet, or are not excelling at the rate you wish, or because you are unclear on the concepts? Then ask yourself if the coach, facilitator, or teacher fits your learning style. Taking ownership of your needs is essential in the learning process, and like everything else in life, it takes time, and practice.

When I first began coaching, I was introduced to the Conscious Competence Theory developed by Noel Burch in the 1970s.[5] It was enlightening for me as a student and a teacher/coach. It helped clarify and give shape to how we learn. Which, in turn, helped me to help my clients name and understand what stage they were experiencing. Having a sense of awareness of where you are at can be a comfort. Learning can be so uncomfortable! It is required that you have faith in yourself, your instructor, and the process. Knowing that you won't be in a constant state of discomfort allows you to endure it, trusting that a shift will come with practice.

I am going to briefly touch on the states of competence in the hopes that it helps you embrace where you are at in your learning process—giving you, in return, a sense of clarity that change will ensue if you continue to apply and practice new skills. The following are my interpretations of Burch's Stages of Learning.

Stage 1: Unconscious Incompetence

During my first year of coaching in Chicago, I was teaching a session on presentation skills at a global consulting firm. In one particular course, when I shared this first stage, one of the participants said point-blank, "I am *not* incompetent." *Touche!* What a great response.

I say that for a few reasons; one, incompetent can be a triggering word, and for this person, it felt inappropriate. I love that they spoke up and said so. It led to me countering with, "How does a state of blissful unawareness sound?" They smiled and said, "that works." Because, indeed, they were unaware of an unconscious habit they had that I then brought to their attention. At first, they were perfectly pleased not to know it. Then, they realized how distracting it was and set on the course of awakening awareness.

Stage 2: Conscious Incompetence

This is where we become cognizant of an area we need to grow.

I liken it to what toddlers experience at the onset of a temper tantrum. It's when we know just enough to get frustrated that we don't know how to execute a new behavior. Whereas kids often have permission to openly express that frustration, we, as adults, are expected to move through it appropriately or sometimes even hold our frustration inside.

For example, have you ever experienced someone giving you feedback on the filler: "um"? As in, someone saying, "Hey, did you realize you said "um" 38 times during your presentation?" At this point, you may start experiencing feelings of disappointment, frustration, and annoyance. (See Stage One. You may have been happier not knowing. Because now you are conscious of something you are not competent in—breathing and pausing between thoughts without an additional vocalization of "um.") Learning how to breathe, pause, and remove that sound will create a more robust and effective delivery of your message.

Oh, the feelings that ensue upon hearing this news! You are now smack in the middle of Stage 2. The next time you present and begin to catch yourself saying, "um," you may feel like having a temper tantrum. That's a reasonable response because you have now entered the state of unlearning an old habit or creating a new one altogether. Neither of which is easy.

New habits take practice.
Conscious practice.

Since we have touched on this specific example, here's some coaching I often give around "um."

Slow your roll. Speak more deliberately. If your pace is too fast, you may not be able to discern what will come out of your mouth next. Fillers, like um, are killers—they can immediately undermine our level of presence.

Take more time to hear what you are saying, and when you feel an "um" coming on, breathe instead.

Hence the next State.

Stage 3: Conscious Competence

This phase is what I like to call "the itchy and scratchy show"[6]

WTF? It's that point in the learning phase where the thing you are working on is like a small insect bite that is healing. It itches on occasion. And when it does, it can be a real bummer. It's where we think, "is this ever going to go away?" And the truth is, it will–with time, patience and practice. When using the sound "um," you must **practice** a few key things:

1. Breathe consciously.
2. Slow your pace of speech.
3. Hear or experience the impulse to utter the sound.
4. Inhibit the sound with either a pause or the use of another word.

Conscious competence is by no means always an uncomfortable state, though. This can also be the phase where you start to find your stride, and give yourself a pat on the back. It's where you are refining your self-awareness to a greater degree through discipline. Your new and more effective habit is taking shape!

Stage 4: Unconscious Competence

Stage 4 occurs when you have practiced a new habit long enough to perform a task effortlessly, with little to no mistakes or thinking around the process.

It is akin to what the late Mihaly Csikszentmihalyi, a distinguished Professor of Psychology and Management, called the state of flow.

"In positive psychology, a flow state, also known colloquially as being in the zone, is the mental state in which a person performing some activity is fully immersed in a feeling of energized focus, full involvement, and enjoyment in the process of the activity."[7]

It may be the case that someone says, "how do you do that?" and you aren't able to account for it because it's baked into your being. It's the payoff for all your hard work! Eloquence and ease. I want to reiterate *with practice*, it is possible in almost every situation.

Take the next few pages to write your takeaways from this chapter, noting what helps you get into a state of flow where your words, actions, message, and feelings are all aligned—moments of "mike drop." I encourage you to do this, especially if your most potent form of learning is writing. Highlight any practice you can explore or continue to enhance moments of flow in your life.

Chapter 2

Breath

Inhale, exhale, pause.
This is how it all begins.
Inhale, exhale, now.

As you read Chapter 1, it may have begun to dawn on you that I am leaning into the notion of breathing—a lot. Breath has become a billion-dollar industry in recent years. Yoga, Mindfulness. Meditation. Millions of people are now investing in learning how to breathe and for a good reason. Breath is the literal foundation for all we do.

I take it so seriously that I have the Kanji symbol for breath[8] tattooed on the back of my neck so that when I turn away from my clients, it's the last thing they see. It's my final reminder to *BREATHE*!

Congratulations. Since you are reading this book, you are, in fact, breathing and thus a terrific candidate for presence training.

The question I have for you is:

How <u>conscious</u> are you of your breathing?

Take a moment right now, and note how you are breathing. The irony is not lost on me that I sometimes struggle with mindful, efficient breathing techniques. So much so that once, when being tested at the Mayo Clinic, I was shocked to see my breath was rapid, shallow, and not in the least bit efficient.

Take two minutes to notice your breathing pattern, then jot down the qualities. Is it shallow? Are you inhaling through your nose or mouth? How far down in your body can you feel movement as you inhale? What does an exhalation feel like for you?

Breath is an involuntary process, and it's a tremendous gift to breathe freely and easily, as I hope you are doing now. Taking your breath from being involuntary (and perhaps inefficient) to purposeful can be *the* most impactful step you take in terms of your presence.

It's no wonder apps like *Calm* and *Headspace* have skyrocketed in the past few years and that mediation isn't just a buzzword for a few practitioners of Zen. Rather it is a worldwide sensation that more and more people are awakening to as a daily practice that enhances their well-being. It's innately connected to the practice of consciously inhaling and exhaling. In other words:

Don't forget to breathe!

Now that you have, in all likelihood, taken a conscious breath, how do you feel? I'd like to take a moment to teach you one of the most simple yet profound exercises I know. It is called "The Whispered Ah." My mentor, Jim Hancock, taught this in a movement course (The Alexander Technique) while pursuing my Master of Fine Arts in Acting at the University of Texas at Austin.

After you read these instructions, close your eyes and give the following a try:

First, make sure you are seated so that you can take a deep full breath; it helps if you adjust your posture. (I will go into this in more depth in Chapter 3.)

Next, place your feet flat on the floor. Get your pelvis underneath your torso, lengthen up through your spine, and lean ever so slightly forward. This gives your body more space to support the breath you will be taking in and, in turn, exhaling out.

Once you've made that adjustment, take a full breath through your nose. The warming action of inhalation through the nose helps calm our parasympathetic nervous system more deeply than a breath through the mouth.

Inhale for five gentle counts, then slowly and easily release a whispered sound of "ah." Note that by releasing the sound "ah," you have to release your lower jaw.

Have you ever noticed in the movies when a person is tense or angry, there is almost always a close-up of their jaw, tensing? There is a reason for this—we hold tension with that powerful hinge. Our jaw is akin to a trap. If we don't release it, it clamps down and holds breath and emotion inside us. By relaxing this set of muscles, you also allow your body to release the emotions and energy within you.

You don't, however, have to speak. You can simply release a conscious, quiet breath that, in turn, helps you to relate whatever feelings you may be experiencing. The "ah" is not to be confused with a sigh. The "ah" is even more gentle. Think of it as the soft, rushing sound of an ocean wave on a calm day. Again, no voice needs to be attached to it. Although if you want a more significant release, you certainly can make a louder "ah"—

but know this—it gets weird in meetings if you start saying "ah" out loud at seemingly random moments.

In Sanskrit, the sound "ah" means "to be." And, according to Buddhist teachings, "ah" is "the seed vowel of our Primordial Wisdom Nature, the very ground of being."[9]

I like knowing that by breathing consciously, allowing the sound of the "ah" to escape, you are connecting with a profound and ancient state of existence.

Releasing tension, releasing any emotions that may not serve you if you act on them or put them into language, helps you connect with your best, most aware, and essential sense of self.

"Ah" is also a sound that is traditionally associated with ease. It has other beneficial impacts, too: "Ahhh, that's over." (Relief.) "Ahhh, a tall cold one…" (Anticipation.)"Ahhh, I see what you are saying." (Connection.) "Ahhh! I get it."(Enlightenment.)

Now that you have the basic concept, I'd like you to take three whispered "ahs"s in a row. I like inhaling for five counts, breathing out for seven, then inhaling again for five, and so on.

I like this count for two reasons. It was how a friend in the eighth grade first taught me mindful breathing. To help me relax before I went on stage for a school play, my friend Sue taught me the 5-7-5 count.

I was only twelve years old, and it's stuck with me for life. Something about that rhythm spoke to me. She also taught me to close off one nostril at a time with a gentle touch of a fingertip. Alternating the pattern. By the time my cue came, I was ready!

Years later, as I began writing in earnest and exploring poetry, I realized what she taught me was the rhythm of a haiku. 5-7-5. Poetry in motion. Ultimately I want you to find a rhythm that works for you. If 5-7-5 works, if it helps you achieve a sense of release and calm, then terrific—continue with it. If another rhythm works for you, go for that.

There is no right or wrong in this. It is about awakening your conscious self and releasing tension and emotion that don't serve you or your audience.

It's about being in the moment.

It centers and grounds you. It prepares you to speak and take action, should action be necessary.

But breath isn't just an upper respiratory affair.

Breath is a full-bodied experience. Have you ever watched a child or animal breathe? It's almost like observing gentle bellows. Their diaphragm rises and falls. Seeing them do this can create a sense of hypnotic well-being in us, the observer. The breath expands not just into the front of the body but into the back.

Our lungs are cylinders. They are huge organs and quite extraordinary.

Have you looked at a map of the Amazon River? Tropical rainforests are called the lungs of the world for a reason. The rainforests surrounding the Amazon River are like the alveoli in our lungs. Each tree is a precious resource that contributes to the production of clean air.

When we breathe to our fullest capacity, we re-oxygenate our bodies and thus both calm and energize ourselves.

A full breath, where we expand into both our belly and our back, sends a message to the rest of our being that we are in a state of readiness. Our awareness increases, and our anxiety decreases.

A study in Great Britain concluded that a presenter/performer's heartbeat synchronizes with that of their audience.

Through their research, they discovered *a direct correlation between the breath and rhythm of a speaker with their audience.* [10] These studies have proven that if your heartbeat is calm and your breath steady, your audience also falls into that rhythm over time.

The inverse is also true. If your heart rate is erratic and you are stressed out, that can spill over onto your audience. Or perhaps you are focused, energized, and inspired, which can also carry over through your breath and heart rate and ripple out and affect your listeners. That's fascinating to contemplate, isn't it?

By centering yourself, you can help center others, which in turn allows your audience to digest your message more fully.

You have the opportunity to impact yourself and others by conscious breath alone.

Let's explore that for a moment.

On your next inhalation, imagine your throat as a channel to a lake, and your spine is a dock on that lake. The incoming air is like water that flows outward toward the shores (the outer edge of your lungs). When you exhale, it comes crashing gently toward the dock of your spinal cord and then recedes up the channel of your throat for a fresh supply.

Inhale, and feel the "water" expand and contract.

Once you get this image, you'll begin consciously filling your lungs (the lake). You can begin actively concentrating on sending that air to various other places in the vast lake of your lungs.

Try sending the breath down into the bottom of your lungs. As your lungs expand downward, your diaphragm will be pushed gently into your abdomen. That's why this is called belly breathing. Your belly will pooch outward, just like babies' do. Allow that space to be filled. Don't worry. Belly breath won't cause any sort of slackness. It's a form of exercise. Feel the belly move out, concentrate, and see if you can experience the inverse. As the diaphragm moves upward, the abdomen will hollow out.

This action is what the practice of Pilates relies on—it is an intimate connection to your core. If you breathe well, you strengthen your body in the process.

Once you've gotten a feel for belly breathing, try something even more in-depth. Try breathing into your back!

Then return to the initial image of your spine as a dock and breathe deeply into your sides. Concentrate on one side at a time. You can direct your breath to various quadrants of your lungs. Try sending breath to the upper right section of your lungs—see if that doesn't help expand and relieve shoulder strain held there. If you are experiencing grief, focus on sending more oxygen up to the left upper quadrant into your heart!

See if you have different reactions to the different types of breathing. Note if one area needs more attention.

Lastly, visualize and target your breath toward certain body parts like your neck, glutes, or hands. Places where breath doesn't literally go to when you breathe. Observe if that helps release any tension held there on your exhale.

There is a primal flow in our breath. It is an ebb and flow. It is rhythmic and soothing and empowers us when we become attuned to it.

Be sure to track if different emotions come up for different placements. Notice how your overall awareness is increasing.

Note if your blood pressure has decreased and if the jungle of your mind has, in turn, quieted.

Know that by practicing mindful breathing, directing it, and getting in touch with the sensations, you are connecting with yourself in a new way. The nervous system gets a break from active stimuli. You are giving yourself a guided tour, and no instructor is necessary. You will know where to go. You will find flow.

One last bit of instruction here, which I will also attribute to my mentor, Jim, is that of "thinking a smile." When I say, "think a smile," frequently, people just smile. But *thinking* a smile is even a bit less energy than a full smile. When you learn to "think a smile," three beautiful things occur. One, the sides of your lips curve slightly upward. You know the phrase, "turn that frown upside down?"[11] That is what thinking a smile does.

Have you ever looked closely at statues of the Buddha or other spiritual figures? They often have a beatific expression on their face. Their mouths curved slightly upward, and their eyes have a bright, easy quality.

One other thing we can't see is your soft palate raises when you think a smile. That's a beneficial action that creates more space for a resonant voice. It's like the diaphragm, an inward working muscle, and when consciously activated, it allows more energy to flow through your body. It creates sensations of vitality and ease. It is not only toned. It *creates* tone and allows for more modulation in the voice. Which, in turn, means you will be more expressive. And ultimately, more connected to yourself and others.

To round out this chapter, I'd like to touch on the power of the pause. A pause is most effective when paired with an inhalation following it and then exhaling as you speak your next thought.

The pause allows you and your audience to digest what you have said. While they continue to digest, your mind is already moving to the next thought. Give them the time to take in your ideas properly. It's a very generous act. You may feel vulnerable at first taking this extra time. However, the payoff is quite extraordinary.

If you are perplexed about when to pause—follow the punctuation! That is why it is there. It visually guides us as to when an author wants you to stop. Reflect. Take a moment and consider, did the period after "reflect" *cause* you to reflect? When speaking, you need to honor the impulses and feelings that come with punctuation. Let those be your guide. Between every new idea—pause and breathe.

When offering a list of things, pause between the items, and offer each one up uniquely so that it can be distinguished from what has gone before and what will follow it.

Every living thing needs oxygen to perform at optimum levels. You are no exception.

Next, create one simple, achievable action plan to help you breathe consciously. Use the space provided to describe that plan and list situations where you will implement that practice.

Revisit these pages in a few weeks and ask yourself how you are doing with the practice. Are there benefits? Or would you like to try another tactic?

Chapter 3

Posture

Lengthen through your head
Lift your heart up, breathe, expand
Feel your spine align.

Our lifestyles have become increasingly sedentary, and one of the many repercussions is our posture de-evolving. Tech neck, iHunch, and good old slouching are becoming more and more routine. I call it C spine. Think about it. When you are sitting, if someone sees you from the side, your body may look curved like the letter C of the English Alphabet.

Your head and neck are rounded often because you are leaning over your technology of choice. In turn, your chest collapses (technically, that collapse is called kyphosis). Your lower back/lumbar area is also rounded, and your pelvic cavity is tipped upward, pointing unnaturally toward your forehead. If you are spending thousands of dollars seeking chiropractic work, this posture may be the culprit!

Like breathing, there is a simple but not necessarily easy fix.

It's what I call C Spine to T Spine. (Side note: while I am aware the natural shape of an aligned spine is a gentle S, for the sake of simplicity, and to help you put these visualizations into practice, I am using the image of the letter T).

Try the following:

First, when sitting, if you can, place your feet flat on the floor. The action of grounding your feet connects and stabilizes you. It helps root and center you.

Second, shift your pelvis back to underneath your torso. This creates alignment through your mid-section freeing your internal organs to support your breath pattern.

Third, lengthen up through your spine (this forms the base of the T.) Then gently lift your heart up. Next, move your shoulders back and down your spine. (This forms the top of the T.)

Then, take a few whispered "ahs" or your breath pattern of choice.

How do you feel?

The singer-songwriter Neil Diamond has a tune with a refrain, "Turn on your heartlight."[12] I love thinking about that as an image. Similar phrases are often used in yoga and personal training.

Growing up Catholic, I also heard that phrase *every* time I went to church.[13] But it wasn't until I was in college when the priest saying the Mass said it in such a powerful way that *I got it*—to lift my heart up was a gentle but firm command for me to literally and figuratively lift my heart and be in a state of reciprocity.

When you physically raise your heart up—allowing your shoulders to shift back, you place yourself in a paradoxical position—you are at once both very vulnerable and equally powerful.

Your body supports itself in the fullest fashion when your posture is upright and aligned. While getting certified to teach Pilates, I learned that if you gently squeeze your scapula together, that is another way to open the chest cavity.

Whatever the means of getting there, a lifted, open heart is the ticket to powerful posture. It's what I call "instant gravitas."

The body never lies.

Martha Graham (one of the 20th Century's most celebrated dancers and choreographers) often shared a story of being caught in a lie by her father when she was a young girl. When she asked her father how he knew it was not the truth, he simply said, "The body never lies."[14]

What I'd like you to consider is that your body, your posture, whether you are aware of it or not, tells a story.

It is a story that always possesses some seeds of innate truth.

Shakespeare said it even more poetically in *Othello*:

Our bodies are gardens, to the which our wills are gardeners.[15]

Get in touch with your body's wisdom. It can teach you powerful lessons, not in how to deceive others, but rather in how to align your thoughts, feelings, and, ultimately, the values that drive you.

What I'd like you to ask yourself is, now that you are in all likelihood working from home or heavily reliant on technology for your day-to-day communication: what truth is your body telling *you*? What message do you think it's saying to *others*?

Are you getting more headaches from Zoom, or some other virtual platform, hour after hour, even if it's for fun and socializing? Does your back ache, or are you catching yourself in the mirror or on your screen, scowling? A classic eye roll tells a very different picture than what you might be saying or not saying with your words.

And the word right now is that people working from home are working *more* than they did when they went into an office.[16] Much emotion and physical tension can build up around that extra call to action.

The truth about your body might be positive as well. Perhaps you are smiling more, your home may be an unexpected haven, and dressing casually allows a type of freedom you didn't experience in a suit or in heels. In turn, you may feel more balanced or are breathing more deeply. Maybe you feel less fatigue because you aren't rushing as much.

This seismic shift in work routines over a few years has granted many of us sizeable opportunities to observe ourselves in a whole new habitat. Your body, if you look and listen to it carefully, is sharing some powerful truths with you. Under every bodily reaction, there is an emotional undercurrent that can guide you toward greater well-being and fuller self-expression.

My work as a coach is about creating synchrony with your mind, body, and spirit. If your body isn't aligned, chances are something isn't quite in harmony, which means the message you are sending to others is, at best, mixed.

For now, try this quick inventory:

Where is your tongue? A crazy question, I know! But if it's plastered against the roof of your mouth, or pressed against your front teeth, that creates a lot of excess tension in your jaw and throat. That action can lead to tension headaches and holding your breath, which inhibits your thought process and, thus, free and natural speech.

Your tongue holds many clues to what's occurring in other parts of your body. Paying attention to it can be helpful in terms of your overall presence and the impression you leave on others.

What story are your shoulders telling? Are they raised or collapsed? Remember, by releasing your shoulders down, lifting your sternum, and gently drawing your shoulder blades together, you will expose more of your heart. This leads you to more connected conversations, leaving a stronger impression of gravitas and, yes, presence.

How are your digits? Check in with your fingers, toes, wrists, and ankles. They have the potential to carry a vast amount of tension, and a quick stretch of the foot or hand can do you a world of good. It can also help you identify what specific feelings you are experiencing (frustration can end up in tense toes and calf muscles, and anxiety often shows up in your fingers).

Releasing tension in the body first, even releasing areas like your ankles, can ease your speech and demonstrate to others that you are entirely in command, at ease, or both.

When you check in with your body, you may realize you need to take a walk or stretch and simply reset yourself altogether. Which, in turn, gives others a chance to do the same as well.

If you are working online, I strongly encourage you to take more breaks. It tends to be more sedentary and yet also rather intense. Set a timer on your phone or smartwatch to remind you to get up and move around each hour. More and more people are finding that stepping away for brief periods helps make them more productive.

Take some time, and open your awareness to the story of your body. It never lies, and the truth it's telling you might just set you free. Writing about your insights and any observations of others' postural lives that impact their overall presence can be helpful too.

Here are a few prompts:

When I see someone slumped at their desk in a meeting, the impact or impression is

_____

_____

When a speaker has an easy, open, lengthened posture, I think

_____

_____

If I see myself in the mirror and I am scowling, what's the impression that leaves on me? What might it leave upon others? (It's the perfect time to *think a smile,* and see what changes.) What other thoughts do you have?

43

Chapter 4

Gesture

To discover flow
You must practice stillness first
Then impulse will know

In the play *Hamlet*, William Shakespeare wrote,

Suit the action to the word and the word to the action.[17]

It was an acting lesson Hamlet was providing to the players (actors) who were to perform a show enacting his father's death. To my way of thinking, it is the most distilled acting lesson ever provided. And it sums up my approach to gestures.

For the record, after years of teaching and coaching voice and speech, I now consider voice to be a gesture. It's a new thought that came to me in recent years.

Our voice, like our movement, becomes more refined with attention and deliberation.

Here I will draw on the system called Laban Movement Analysis.[18] Rudolf Laban came up with the following "effort elements,"[19] and it's clear they apply to both movement and speech.

This is my distilled approach to Laban's more complex system. I find it makes for easy vocabulary when thinking about how to move and speak and I hope you do, too.

First, there are the efforts: Space, Weight, Time, and Flow.
Here are the elements that fall into the efforts:

SPACE: Direct/Indirect
WEIGHT: Strong/Light
TIME: Sudden/Sustained
FLOW: Bound/Free

The genius is in its simplicity; once you understand the basics, a world of movement and vocal modulation opens up.

More specifically, for vocal work, I find incorporating these other descriptors that address volume and tone helpful:

Loud/Soft
Definitive/Questioning
Warm/Shrill
Breathy/Grounded
Hoarse/Smooth
Nasal/Resonant
Muddled/Crisp

Your voice, like a gesture, is something that you can almost always positively alter if you pay attention to it, and deliberately work on it.

Your movement and vocal quality must align with your words so the message is crystal clear.

While these descriptions are all well and good, the question is how do we get to a place of deliberate gesture and tone, pitch and diction, and achieve authenticity simultaneously?

Here we can take a tip from athletes who practice and performing artists who rehearse. There is no way through it but to do it. You can't think or visualize your way through this process.

The best tactic is to tackle one thing at a time.[20]

The first practice I suggest to almost all my clients is stillness. Being still in front of a group for 30 seconds is one of the most daunting things! It truly gets down to the very essence of our being, which can feel very vulnerable.

Many people have asked me over the years, "...but what do I do with my arms?" And my reply is, "Let them just hang by your side until you feel the impulse to move them."

Only some people are willing to take the time to be still and allow impulses to guide them. For me, this was the most authentic way to sense my instincts and movement patterns. For others, it can be a more time-consuming process or frustrating (thirty to sixty seconds can feel like an eternity!) or not in agreement with their primary learning style, so that's when I, as a coach, will pivot to another technique.

For most of us, we simply have excess energy coursing through our bodies, and energy has to go somewhere. It gets channeled into some type of fidgety movement. Here are a few examples: twisting a ring on a finger, twirling the hair, side stepping, or pushing weight into one hip. If you have a pen in your hand, you may point it, or worse yet—constantly click it!

We make thousands of moves a day. But here's the question—are they in support of your verbal message? If not, then you need to discover what physical habits you have.

Here's where technology, and a good friend or a professional presence coach, pay off. Each can help you identify your habits.

If you have Zoom, a smartphone, or a video camera, record yourself either just standing and experiencing stillness, or if you have a presentation coming up use that, then play it back. Ask your inner critic to leave the room first; then take the sound off, and watch your gestures. What is your face saying? Are your arm movements distracting? Is there a vibrancy in your posture? Next, turn the visual element off and simply listen. Listen as you would to a podcast. Are the right words and concepts being cued up?

Then try it again. Applying these different techniques:

First, consider: how you want your audience to *feel* receiving your message. (If you answer "informed," ask yourself why you aren't just sending an email).

To clarify verbal messaging and up your overall presence simultaneously, I encourage presenters to choose a *physically active verb* that will lead the audience to a new emotional state. (Informing is a cerebral word but not highly physical or active.) Think about that for a moment, and if you need help thinking of active verbs, do a quick Google search. Then do some writing–or moving, depending on your learning style as you **answer the following questions:**

How are your voice and body different if you try to *persuade* someone instead of *challenging* or *reassuring* them?

What qualities make up an *inspiring* delivery? Get very specific in your answer here. How does the voice sound? The volume, pace, pitch, and tone? And what physical gestures accompany inspiration?

If you are stumped, look up a few Ted Talks under the heading "inspirational" because speakers have very different styles. Look at a Brené Brown video; then check out Tony Robbins. Their approaches couldn't be more different. Yet, both fill the stage with presence and, more often than not, tremendous inspiration.

You may come back from watching and say one was uplifting and the other was compelling. If so—discern the difference. Start to break it down. How specifically is uplifting a listener different from compelling them?

Eye contact is a gesture that can aid your audiences in feeling connected to you. Applying intentionality and Laban to your eye contact can significantly impact your presence. Some say the eyes are the window to the soul. That said, light, direct eye contact, where you wait to see or receive a cue as to whether or not to sustain the look from the person you are speaking to or with, is an excellent general guideline in North American Business culture. Be sure to ask what the norms are regarding eye contact in any culture outside your own, then adjust accordingly.

When delivering a presentation, you need to be intentional. And invest in it emotionally. When you are intentional, your body and voice shift, and there's a greater possibility that your message will be clear from head to toe and resonate visually, auditorily, and verbally with the audience. Physically and vocally, practicing intention can have a tremendous impact on you, your audience, and how they feel about your message. If you invest in it, chances are more significant that the audience will too.

Start looking up active verbs, and start applying them: *today!*

Next, use your body and voice in the way Laban would. Nobody is watching you, so go outside your comfort zone!

Try applying any of the eight effort actions (combinations of the movement elements and efforts) to your message:

Punch
Slash
Dab
Flick
Press
Wring
Glide
Float

Try pressing a point home. Pressing is *direct, strong, and sustained*. Do it vocally first, then try a gesture. When you float an idea by someone, often you get lighter vocally, and your movements may be more fluid. The floating effort is *light, indirect, and free*.

Applying the effort of gliding, which is *direct, light, and sustained,* can be very helpful if you have a staccato rhythm to your speech.

By staccato, I mean short bursts of thought, two to three words at a time, that break up the meaning of your idea. It's like repetitively *dabbing* each word. And it can sound a bit robotic after a while, and *gliding* and *floating* can give your speech a legato (more melodic) quality which is

56

more soothing and engaging. And in general, a better fit for long-flowing ideas.

Let's return to some earlier questions about motivation and inspiration under the lens of Laban.

Are motivating actions stronger and more direct? Is inspiration lighter and sustained? Record yourself trying out those two different approaches. Observe. See it for yourself. Continue rehearsing it, feeling it in your body, expressing it in your voice. Find ways that are true to your form. Find movement and vocal patterns that support the circumstances you are in.

Watching and listening to yourself can be difficult. It's important to note you don't hear yourself the way others do, nor do you see yourself the same way.

So, ask a friend or colleague, *someone you trust,* and who you can share what you specifically want feedback on—someone who will share it clearly and succinctly without *shoulding* on you.

My mentor, Jim Hancock, used to say,

Stop shoulding on yourself.

Shoulding on yourself? That's right. Don't should upon yourself or others.

The word 'should' can have an unpleasant effect. A good coach or colleague knows this—they make suggestions, ask probing questions, and allow you to do the practice rather than talking you through every detail.

Lastly, they shy away from saying, "you should do this." Because the truth is there is no one perfect way of executing something–only practicing new things until you embody them authentically and with ease and flow.

What about this chapter piqued your interest?

Did you try any of the suggestions? Does it make you want to engage a coach? If so, use this space to list what you want to focus on. Remember, the more specific you can be, the better you will be able to discern if the potential coaches you are interviewing are a good fit.

Chapter 5

Content

Your language matters
Devise a loose script and trust
Less is often more

This chapter could get very lengthy! In the spirit of distilling, I will touch on three key points—filler words, vocabulary, and concision.

All of it comes down to, as Shakespeare once wrote:

Words, words, words[21]

One of the biggest challenges I face in coaching is the inundation of filler words and phrases.

When it comes to content that distracts listeners, you may have caught this earlier in Chapter 2:

Filler is Killer

What exactly do I mean by filler?

I call fillers "no value add" sounds, words, and phrases that distract from and deflate your penultimate message.

Here's a list of some common ones. See if any of them resonate for you as a listener or a speaker:

Um, er, so, kind of, you know, right, absolutely, like, basically, really, seriously, actually, OK, totally, you know what I mean, honestly, just, very, however, as far as I'm concerned, at the end of the day, probably, maybe, completely, and things like that,

This list is by no means exhaustive. Almost anything can become a filler.

Even saying "I think" can be a filler because by the very virtue that you are saying it, a listener can conclude you also think it. It may also be your way of prefacing something to hedge your bet instead of declaring it and taking a risk.

To drive this point home, try reading this passage out loud:

So, um, what I think is that filler words are kind of, you know, not necessary. I absolutely get that words matter. Like, think about it, OK?. Basically, these words and phrases take up extra space. Right? Seriously, this is something you should actually think about and really work on. It's a totally worthy exploration to remove them from your vocabulary. You know what I mean? Honestly, it's just very, very practical. And an important step in upping your presence. As far as I am concerned, it's actually critical. And at the end of the day, it will probably be a complete game-changer for you. Maybe it will even gain you a promotion and things like that. Either way, when you remove them, they can completely change how others receive you.

Did you recognize any habits there?

Now try saying this:

Filler words are not necessary. They can change how others perceive you.

That was the key message that was hidden amidst all the filler.

Filler comes into play when we lack awareness and aren't listening to ourselves. It also occurs when we are outpacing ourselves. (Again, head back to Chapter 2 on breath if you need to work on pace!)

You have to slow your pace to hear what you are saying. You also often need an outside resource to help you listen to what you are missing.

While there is new AI technology that can record you and count all your words, taking you from unconscious incompetence to consciousness, you must ask yourself, can AI help me through the learning phases of conscious competence with compassion?

If AI is your jam, by all means, employ it to assess what fillers you are using.

After, try utilizing the human touch with this technique, developed alongside my husband when we worked together with a CEO named John in Chicago.

Every time John said, "you know," one of us said the word "banana." It was hilarious and daunting!

I have used it several times over the years, and people just start laughing at themselves. It also drives home the need to slow down to hear the sounds and words that have become a part of both our musical memory and, thereby, have become potentially undermining or distracting habits.

John ultimately gave his team permission also to use "banana" every time he said "you know," and he said that within two weeks, he was no longer using the phrase.

One other place where a filler can be a killer is when we reply to people, "That's a great question." This response can get tricky because if said too often, it becomes disingenuous. It also may not be a good question, in which case your saying so is an outright lie.

How, then, can you approach this tricky situation?

First and foremost, take a moment to breathe. Simply allow there to be silence as you think.

Consider the following wisdom from Shakespeare's *Romeo & Juliet:*

Wisely and slow, they stumble that run fast.[22]

By taking more time before speaking (what may at first feel as if you are going far too slowly), the chances of you outpacing yourself lessen.

Here are verbal responses you can also try:

Thank you, I appreciate your asking that...

I wasn't anticipating this question...

I need a moment to consider that.

I don't have an answer for you right now.

> (After that last statement, offer a follow-up to get them the answer or connect them with who does.)

Saying "I don't know" isn't a commentary on your entire persona or body of knowledge. It's an honest response. If necessary, refer people to another time to discuss the topic or to the person who has the answer. I'll touch on this more when it comes to the chapter on mindset.

Once you know your fillers, my following questions center around how your intentional messages are landing.

When you speak, how does your audience typically respond? Are they engaged? What signals tell you they are engaged?

How often do you think about that?

Our words matter. The vocabulary we choose to express ourselves tells a lot about us and shapes the impression we leave upon others.

Lately, I am hearing a great many war metaphors.

The current crises unleashed upon the world are harrowing. The pandemonium of illness, war, climate change, and political divide are in and of themselves devastatingly real and cruel adversaries.

I actively advocate that leaders shift their mindset and language away from "fighting" and "taking up arms against" the upheaval we are facing.

I suggest another paradigm altogether. One Shakespeare touched on beautifully within his play *Henry V.*

In the famous speech that begins, "Once more unto the breach, dear friends. Once more...." Henry and his beleaguered forces were facing a bloody fight against the French at Agincourt.[23] So, the battleground language is apt.

But something like the coronavirus or financial collapse is an altogether different kind of foe.

When I dig deeper into Henry's words and distill them, I believe he calls forth an even more potent and definitive directive than "to stiffen the sinews or summon up the blood."

Early on, he says,

In peace, there is nothing, so becomes a man
As modest stillness and humility.

Gender aside—as a leader, you shift your perspective and view things from the standpoint that underlying all this disruption (whatever it be) is "Peace."

Set aside the many bold and bloody metaphors that Henry V uses, step outside the mindset of battle, and you will discover these telltale lines:

...bend up every spirit—To his full height

"Bending up the Spirit" comes through the action of breathing and "To his full height" directly implies posture *does* matter!

Later in the passage, Henry follows by speaking this brilliant and compelling call to action:

The game's afoot:
Follow your spirit.

If you see any situations you are facing as a metaphorical war, I encourage you to shift your paradigm to that of PEACE and tend to your SPIRIT. Now. Do so to your full height.

Here are ideas on how to do that:

- Meditate or Pray. Or both if they are somehow different for you.

- Take time and take stock of your values. Write them down. Then ask your spouse or partner if you are living up to them. Then ask a colleague.

- Set the intention of instilling peace, reassurance, or loving communication before a call. Yes, I did just use the word love. Because I believe it feeds the spirit. If you don't believe in the spirit, consider that it's simply time to breathe and collect yourself, and reflect.

- Go for a walk in Nature, alone, in silence before or after your calls.

- When you don't know the answer to something, admit it.

- Ask for help when you need it.

- Apologize when you have lost your cool or wronged someone.

- Take care of your body. Stand and sit up straight. Allow space for your spirit to move through your body with ease. Practice breathing consciously and more deeply.

- Turn all your electronic devices off and just be with yourself or your family. But choose. Taking time for yourself is essential, as is time with your family. But they are vastly different. Be clear on what you are doing and when.

- Take time to write out what you are grateful for—then tell people individually, in short notes or face to face, how much you appreciate them. Treat colleagues like friends.

- Set time aside for one-on-one follow-up conversations with people rather than being on large group calls.

- Shorten your meetings whenever possible.

- Be mindful of the metaphors you use and their impact on your audience.

- Choose to use more interesting, rich, and situationally specific vocabulary. (If a colleague or team member gives an exceptional presentation, instead of saying, "That was great," tell them it was exceptional or outstanding, Then back it up with specifics: "You connected with the audience through your eye contact. Your three key points were clear and concise. I always appreciate that I can hear every word you say," etc.)

- Practice your emotional intelligence (EQ)[24] by checking in with others and expressing your current feeling state (in appropriate settings) when things don't quite resonate. (i.e., consider letting people know you are frustrated rather than keeping it all in and having them (possibly) misread your silence or stony face.)

- Actively seek places and people with whom you can openly share new ideas and paradigms as you move with greater tranquility, not into the fray, but into the future.

- Buy a thesaurus, or use one online, and strive to enhance your vocabulary. Consider what new or heightened words you can use to connect with others authentically.

The game *is* afoot, and as a leader, following your spirit is essential for our collective well-being, the ultimate win, and greater peace prevailing.

Take the following few pages to take notes on the following questions:

What kind of metaphors and visual language are you using?

What do you think the impact of those words, or lack thereof is on others?

Remember, your language impacts people's perception of you and what you are saying. In turn, it affects your overall presence.

Lastly, I want to offer a few thoughts on being quiet and concise, starting with another quote from *Henry V*:

Men of few words are the best men.[25]

I love this quote for several reasons, but primarily because it describes my husband to a T. He is a man of few words. That is not to say he is shy because he is not. He simply appreciates silence and adds to conversations when he chooses. Jeremy is not one to needlessly reiterate other people's thoughts, nor does he talk simply to hear the sound of his own voice.

What I find fascinating about his silence is how it affects other people. Frankly, a lot of people are uncomfortable with quiet companions. Quiet people are often considered aloof or even arrogant. Some people experience, in the shadow of a quiet person's silence, they are being judged. When in fact, that's often the farthest thing from the truth. He is simply listening actively, which is rare these days.

Hence, people 'of few words' often get the feedback that they need to talk more at meetings.

When I coach people, sometimes I have to get creative for them to stay true to their quiet nature while at the same time heeding the feedback and learning to speak up.

How? There are a few important notions I point out to 'quiet' clients.

Because the business culture in the U.S. values vocal opinions, being silent can, and will often, be misconstrued. One of the first tactics is to encourage clients to get into the mindset of "when in Rome..."[26]

The old adage implies we must step outside ourselves and our habits and consider our audiences' culture and needs.

Here I would like to pose this question:

What if those who like to talk were consistently given the feedback to be quiet and listen more? In *King Lear*, Shakespeare wrote:

Have more than you show.
Speak less than you know.[27]

Taking on that paradigm shift in Western culture could be a game-changer!

Speaking less, pausing, and asking more questions instead of deep diving into data or making statements to prove how much you know is a way of inviting dialogue.

Dialogue and conversation are often far more powerful than a monologue or what is called a soliloquy—which is about expressing your thoughts regardless of having an audience.

Keep in mind great presence entails being aware of your audience and responding to them in a genuine way. There is a time and place for all. Listening to your audience and your own impulses is essential.

When we are in "Rome" or any culture outside our comfort zone, I return to the idea of magic and offer a technique based on "The Magic If" developed by the great Russian acting teacher Konstantin Stanislavski.[28] When I was taught it in a workshop by another formidable acting instructor, Stella Adler, she called it "Acting as if."

It's interesting to note the famous Austrian psychologist Arthur Adler also used the phrase "Acting as if" in his therapy.[29] While Arthur and Stela share a surname, they are unrelated—Stella Adler was born into a famous Yiddish acting family in New York. However, the concept they both purported was very similar.

Alfred Adler's concept of the "Acting as if" technique encourages one to begin acting as if they were already the person they would like to be.

Within the world of performance and coaching, it's fairly similar. Use your imagination. First, picture the circumstance you will be in. Note the emotions and physical responses that come up just thinking about it. Then *Act as if* you are someone who speaks a lot or speaks with great authority. If you want, you can even choose someone real, someone you admire. A person who has the type of presence you would like to achieve.

When clients do this and fully commit to it, the change is noticeable. Their experience is palpable. Not only does their voice shift, but their posture also improves, gestures change, *and* they contribute with more gravitas. In short, they feel empowered to own the space!

I want to be clear. "Acting as if" isn't about mimicking or impersonating someone. Instead, it's about envisioning the circumstances that will surround you and trying new qualities, perhaps even new values and intentions, in a way that suits your persona. In doing so, you may begin owning these new qualities.

Instead of calling it faking it until you make it, practice it until it starts to feel natural and authentic. Patience is paramount. Creating a new habit takes time and effort. In time, you will own it. Or you'll discover it simply isn't aligned with your values. Either way, it is a worthy exploration.

A second tactic I employ is this: think in terms of your speaking up as a gift. (The same can be said of gentle eye contact: it can be a gift!)

Although *you* may not feel comfortable being vocal, throwing out a few more ideas may make your *team members or clients* more comfortable. That is truly a great contribution—putting those around you at ease. It is a deliberate act of generosity, and it *will* pay off. The inverse can also be true. If you tend to speak up a lot–or interrupt people–your silence can be a gift!

Finally, as a person of few words, you can add to meetings by posing questions, summarizing ideas, or facilitating. Debating a point can also be the key to chiming in—but take a breath first, then ask yourself if it's an appropriate action for the audience. Listen to your instincts, and be willing to take risks to find the best way to interact.

For example, let's say the vocal contributors get going, and you see the meeting has gone over time or is veering off track. Take that opportunity to point out how things have gotten off track or pose the idea of returning to things after everyone has had a break so that everyone gets some necessary downtime to ponder the issues. Stepping into a meeting in that capacity can be as valuable as throwing out a groundbreaking idea.

At the risk of sounding like a broken record, I want to reiterate, regardless of your natural inclinations to speak or not to speak, before you try any of these ideas, remember to pause, then inhale and exhale. Breath is the essence of inspiration!

If you have the proper support via inhalation, the thought will be more precise, and the sound of your voice will be more robust on the exhalation, guaranteeing you will be heard. If you have trouble interrupting, use some Laban. Press the table to help ground you, and speak up. Or using a slashing gesture (within reason) to cut through the flurry of other ideas being bandied about.

How did this chapter, filled with words, words, words resonate with you?

How do labels and preferences like introversion and extroversion affect your presence or your choices about your delivery? How can you authentically encourage yourself to speak up, speak out, and, as I like to say—pump up the jam by 10% when an audience needs to be not just informed of your data or ideas but awakened by them?[30]

As with previous chapters, take the space provided for your reflections.

Chapter 6

Mindset

Treat yourself with care
Start there. Then find a mantra.
Words can compel you.

As a coach, one of the primary things I work on with my clients is their mindset and developing a personalized mantra that empowers them when self-doubt or their inner critic shows up.

There is nothing either good nor bad but thinking it makes it so.

You guessed it—this is also a quote from Shakespeare.[31] It is from Hamlet's conversation with his childhood friends Rosencrantz and Guildenstern.

Hamlet considers Denmark a prison; Rosencrantz and Guildenstern do not. Hamlet then sums up their disagreement with that quote. I believe it epitomizes the whole ideology behind mantras.

Oftentimes, the reason people hire an executive coach in the first place is that their mindset surrounding their presence is flagging. Their confidence has taken a hit, or their inner critic is nagging them.

In turn, self-doubt is becoming more intrusive and affecting how they appear in the world (i.e., their Presence.)

Some people want to discover the *why* behind their beliefs or behaviors. As a coach, I say, "rather than focusing on *why* it exists, let's focus on *how* to change it."

The *why* often presents itself through the coaching process, and I consider that a happy accident of sorts. Searching for the *why* is one of the critical things that distinguishes coaching from therapy. If you work on *changing* your mindset, then *why* it started in the first place can become a moot point.

Here are some of the mindsets my clients have come in with: "I am no good at public speaking." Or, the classic, "I am afraid of public speaking." "I'm an introvert, and I'm not excelling at client relations." "I'm too old to change at this point." (I think with a mindset like the last one, it's interesting they've employed a coach. It implies there's a second, more positive mindset dueling to be top dog.)

At the start of the coaching process, in addition to asking them how they learn, I also ask my clients how they *feel* regarding what we are working on.

Do you like your current job? Do you believe you're good at what you do? Is there room for improvement? What thoughts run through your head right before a presentation?

It's incredible how many people will answer with statements chock full of fillers, such as, "Well, I'm *kind of* good at it." "Maybe I can improve." Or another variation, "I think I could *sort of* improve." Then, some are really in the trenches with thoughts such as, "I am really bad at this, and I don't know what difference this is going to make."

This may very well sound like a sound bite straight out of Norman Vincent Peale's mouth, who is famous for writing and espousing the Power of Positive Thinking.[32] I am here to tell you, Peale, along with several other inspirational authors, philosophers, and teachers got it right: Your thoughts shape you.

What kind of mantras are out there? There are thousands, and finding the right one for you may take some time and effort. Having a coach or friend helping you discover one can be very helpful because oftentimes, they see your potential through a lens that's blurry for you.

Several years ago, while performing in *Lust Supper*, a play written by Kirk Lynn and produced by the Rude Mechs in Austin, Texas,[33] I went through a period of incredible stage fright. It was so bad that I honestly didn't think I would remember my lines, so I took it upon myself to employ several measures to ensure I could do my job.

The first was physical. Since I am highly kinesthetic (I learn through movement), I opted to go into the show every night over an hour early and run through my blocking (the pattern I move through on stage.) I also went through my lines as often as possible before others started to arrive.

In addition to those techniques, I did one very specific physical action: I took to touching each seat in the theater (it was small!), making sure to connect with the entire space. While these things sound compulsive, the rituals helped calm me, and the touching of the seats reminded me this was ultimately for the audience—not me.

The last and most potent measure I took was to employ a new mantra. As this fear was creeping in and sucking out all of my enjoyment of acting, I gave myself a good talking to—I reminded myself why I was in this show in the first place. I reminded myself that I love acting, and I know how to do it. I had trained for moments just like this. And there it was! My mantra came rolling out. I'd hit on it. "I know how to do this."

That was several years ago, but here's the thing: I still use that mantra today.

It has been one of the most effective tools for bolstering my self-confidence. "I know this. I know how to do it." For the record, I will even say my mantra out loud when I need an even more potent boost.

When my clients hit upon a mantra that works for them, I see some riveting changes in their work. One of the most vivid I recall was when a young consultant seeking focus and passion chose: "I spit hot fire."

Others have taken a much more traditional route and employed Sanskrit mantras, like those utilized in yoga practice: "Om Namah Shivaya,"[34] which very loosely translated means something to the effect of "Om and salutations to that which I am capable of becoming." It has a great rhythm to it, and it works very well with the breathing exercises I give my clients.

Others have included: "I am a leader." "I don't think it. I know it." "No one knows more about this than I do." "I am the expert here." There's also, "I'm ready." And, "I've got this."

For good measure, let's also take one last line from Shakespeare. Perhaps the mantra of all mantras:

This above all,
to Thine Own Self be True.[35]

Here are a few tips to keep in mind when creating a mantra:

1. They are short
2. They are powerful
3. They embolden you
4. They are present tense

Words and images accompany almost every thought, so if the thoughts or images we choose to see and believe weaken or undermine us, we must strive to shift them. As a coach, I believe we have the power to do that.

We must awaken our faith in ourselves, our abilities, and our experience. This is the undercurrent of all authentic presence: a belief in yourself and your abilities. Then fully embodying what you stand for in a way that is fully aligned from your breath to your posture, gestures (voice, facial expressions, and the movements in your limbs), content, and mindset.

The next time your inner critic—or even an outside critic—speaks up and implies you aren't up to the task or aren't capable of hitting a metaphorical home run, see what it's like to shift to a mantra that empowers you.

Given time and practice, you can begin changing things simply by taking a deep breath and contemplating it first.

As for the Five Points—begin where it suits you and how you learn best.

Often clients will ask me for "*the*" way to deliver something. In truth, there is no one way. The only "always" I offer in coaching is to breathe. Consciously breathe; it's where it all starts and where it ends.

The last thing I will leave you with is a poem I wrote, inspired by the Chinese philosopher Lao Tze.[36]

Each stanza is a haiku and distills the Five points of Presence to their barest essence:

First, Breathe, Breathe and Be
Observant of your Body;
Actions Speak Volumes.

Breathe, then take a Pause,
Listen with your Ears and Eyes;
Be Intentional.

Breathe; and be Mindful
of the Thoughts and Images
that Dance in your Head.

Breathe; Practice Gently
Rehearse until you find Flow;
These traits Reveal You.

Breathe; Know Your Presence
Has an Impact Until the–
Final Breath You Take.

Acknowledgements

I am deeply grateful to the Southeastern Minnesota Arts Council (SEMAC) for granting me the time, space, and generous funds to write this book. I am honored to be a working artist here in Lanesboro.

Great thanks go to my dear and loving friend Stef O'Keefe for her editing skills, thoughtful suggestions, attention to detail, and dedication to the Arts. Stef, you honor me every time you remove or add a dash. You keep me on track with your brilliance, diligence, and fabulous sense of humor.

Here's a big shout-out to Sarah Minor for assisting in creating yet another beautiful cover and Joann van Meter for your keen eye and final edits.

Jack Uldrich, you have inspired me since we were kids. It's a blessing having you as a brother, a mentor, a friend, as well as an honest and kind critic. Words alone aren't enough to thank you.

For my husband, Jeremy van Meter, your endless love means the world to me. You are my heart and my home.

To my childhood friend, Sue (Hall) Farley, little did you know how much I learned from you in the sacristy of Saint Thomas. I may owe my entire career to you, teaching me how to breathe.

Lastly, "thanks and ever thanks" to many mentors, teachers, and clients (especially Dean Bell and Saoirse Storey for your kind endorsements and friendship.) And last but in no way least, Jim Hancock, your work has taken me and everyone I work with "onwards and upwards."

About the Author

Catherine Glynn is a leading executive coach and performing artist. She is the Founder and CEO of Voce Veritas—an Executive Leadership and Communications Firm—and the Founder and Artistic Director of A.R.T. (Audacious Raw Theater). She holds a BA in Humanities from the College of St. Benedict and St. John's University and MFAs in Acting from the University of Texas at Austin and The University of Delaware's Professional Theatre Training Program. She is a proud member of the Actor's Equity Association (AEA) and the Screen Actors Guild/American Federation of Television and Radio Artists (SAG/AFTRA). She is also a certified Pilates Instructor. She has authored seven plays, one book of haiku poems called *Small Things*, and *Leadership, Distilled: Twelve Brief Lessons, One Big Impact*. Her coaching practice focuses on helping visionaries on the verge find their true voice. She is also a facilitator and coach with the global coaching firm Ariel based outside of Boston. She regularly works with international consulting firms, C-Suite and senior-level executives, leading business schools, and Non-Profit Directors. Her clients include the Mayo Clinic, SGA Youth and Family Services of Chicago, Harvard Business School, Google, and Yale School of Management, along with other top business schools and Fortune 500 companies.

If you are interested in having her speak to your organization or working with her privately, inquiries may be sent to: info@voceveritas.com.

VoceVeritas.com

Citations

1. Page 7

Oxford Languages & Google citation:
https://www.google.com/search?q=je+ne+sais+quoi&oq=je+ne&aqs=chrome.0.0i512j69i57j0i512j46i512l2j0i512l3j46i512j0i512.4145j1j7&sourceid=chrome&ie=UTF-8

2. Page 7

Shakespeare, William, *As You Like It*, Act II, scene vii

3. Page 10

Shakespeare, William, *The Winter's Tale*, Act V, scene iii, Paulina.

4. Page 15

Suzuki, Shunryu. *Zen Mind, Beginner's Mind: Informal Talks on Zen Meditation and Practice.* Weatherhill, 1970.

5. Page 16

Burch, Noel. *The Theory of Conscious Competence.* Gordon Training International, 1970.

6. Page 19

Groening, Matt, *The Simpsons*, The Itchy & Scratchy Show,
https://en.wikipedia.org/wiki/The_Itchy_%26_Scratchy_Show: *The Itchy & Scratchy Show* (often shortened as *Itchy & Scratchy*) is a fictional

animated television series featured on *The Simpsons* television series, Fox Broadcasting Company. Author note: When coaching and talking about this phase of learning, I often sing the tune of *The Itchy & Scratchy* show out loud for clients, in the same voice used for the theme song.

7. Page 20
Scholarly Community Encyclopedia, Flow State,
https://encyclopedia.pub/entry/28116
Author note: I want to thank my neighbor and friend Michael Brown for introducing me to Mihaly Csikszentmihalyi. This work backed up experiences I had for years but never knew there was precise science around it.

8. Page 23
Kanji symbol for breath/chi:

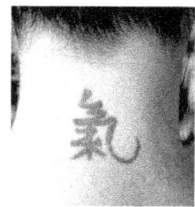

Author note: Huge shout out to my friend Meghan Manzella for encouraging me to get this tattoo from "Chicago's favorite tattooer" Nick Colella.

9. Page 27
The Ah Mantra, https://zenawakened.com/the-ah-mantra/

10. Page 29

Devlin, Richardson, Hogan and Nuttall, UCL Division of Psychological and Language Sciences,

https://www.ucl.ac.uk/pals/news/2017/nov/audience-members-hearts-beat-together-theatre

> "The research led by the UCL Division of Psychological and Language Sciences (PaLS) has found that watching a live theatre performance can synchronize your heartbeat with other people in audience, regardless of if you know them or not. The research was conducted by Dr Joe Devlin, Dr Daniel C. Richardson, John Hogan (all Department of Experimental Psychology) and Dr Helen Nuttall (Lancaster University). The team monitored the heart rates and electro dermal activity of 12 audience members at a live performance of the West End musical *Dreamgirls*. The team found that as well as alongside individuals' emotional responses, the audience members' hearts were also responding in unison, with their pulses speeding up and slowing down at the same rate."

11. Page 32

Author note: I actually hate "turn that frown upside down." Or worse yet, the new acronym, RBF, which stands for Resting Bitch Face. Ugggghhhh! Enough with the sexism! Can we just call it resting face?

12. Page 38

Diamond, Neil, Bayer Sager, Carol, Bacharach, Burt, "Heartlight", Polygon Records, 1982.

Author note: Yet another tune I will happily sing to clients, in my best Neil Diamond imitation (which is comedic at best) as a form of inspiration, or better yet, humor.

13. Page 39

Catholic Mass, Lift up your heart, https://www.catholicdigest.com/amp/faith/spirituality/mass-lift-hearts

14. Page 39

Graham, Martha, *Blood Memory*, Washington Square, 1992.

15. Page 40

Shakespeare, William, *Othello*, Act I, scene iii, Iago.

16. Page 40

Parker, Menasce Horowitz, and Minkin, *COVID-19 Pandemic Continues To Reshape Work in America*, https://www.pewresearch.org/social-trends/2022/02/16/covid-19-pandemic-continues-to-reshape-work-in-america/

17. Page 47

Shakespeare, William, *Hamlet*, Act II, scene ii, Hamlet.

18. Page 48

Laban Movement Analysis, https://labaninstitute.org/about/rudolf-laban/

19. Page 48

Laban Efforts,
https://www.thenarrativeproject.net/wp-content/uploads/2017/03/Laban-Character-development.pdf?x72572

20. Page 49

Glynn, Catherine, Walker, Jewel, *One Thing at a Time.*,
https://www.linkedin.com/pulse/one-thing-time-catherine-glynn/

21. Page 61

Shakespeare, William, *Hamlet*, Act II, scene ii, Hamlet.
    Polonius: What do you read, my lord?
    Hamlet: Words, words, words.
    Polonius: What is the matter, my lord?
    Hamlet: Between who?
    Polonius: I mean, the matter that you read, my lord.
    Hamlet: Slanders, sir: for the satirical rogue says here that old men have grey beards....
    Polonius: [Aside] Though this be madness, yet there is method in't.

22. Page 64

Shakespeare, William, *Romeo and Juliet,* Act II, scene iii, Friar Lawrence.

23. Page 66

Shakespeare, William, *Henry V*, Henry V, Act III, scene i, Henry
https://poets.org/poem/henry-v-act-iii-scene-i-once-more-unto-breach-
dear-friends Author note: If you want to hear this spoken, Kenneth
Branagh does a badass version of it in his movie rendition of "Henry V"
released in 1989.

Once more unto the breach, dear friends, once more;

Or close the wall up with our English dead!

In peace there's nothing so becomes a man,

As modest stillness and humility;

But when the blast of war blows in our ears,

Then imitate the action of the tiger:

Stiffen the sinews, conjure up the blood,

Disguise fair nature with hard-favoured rage:

Then lend the eye a terrible aspect;

Let it pry through the portage of the head,

Like the brass cannon; let the brow o'erwhelm it

As fearfully as doth a galled rock

O'erhang and jutty his confounded base,

Swill'd with the wild and wasteful ocean.

Now set the teeth and stretch the nostril wide;

Hold hard the breath and **bend up every spirit**

To his full height. On, on, you noblest English,

Whose blood is fet from fathers of war-proof!

Fathers that, like so many Alexanders,

Have in these parts from morn till even fought,

And sheathed their swords for lack of argument.

Dishonour not your mothers: now attest,

That those whom you call'd fathers did beget you.

Be copy now to men of grosser blood,

And teach them how to war. And you, good yeoman,

Whose limbs were made in England, show us here

The mettle of your pasture: let us swear

That you are worth your breeding; which I doubt not;

For there is none of you so mean and base,

That hath not noble lustre in your eyes.

I see you stand like greyhounds in the slips,

Straining upon the start. **The game's afoot:**

Follow your spirit; and upon this charge,

Cry 'God for Harry! England! and Saint George!'

24. Page 69

EQ | Emotional Intelligence

The term was first coined in 1990 by researchers John Mayer and Peter Salovey, but was later popularized by psychologist Daniel Goleman.

https://online.hbs.edu/blog/post/emotional-intelligence-in-leadership

25. Page 73

Shakespeare, William, *Henry V*, Henry V, Act III, scene ii, Boy.

26. Page 74

When in Rome...

https://en.wikipedia.org/wiki/When_in_Rome,_do_as_the_Romans_do

Author note: This is a fascinating story about the origin of this centuries old proverb. It started with three saints. Which leads me to believe at some point I ought to write a joke, "Three saints walked into a bar…"

27. Page 74
Shakespeare, William, *King Lear*, Act I, scene iv, Lear.

28. Page 75
Mroczka, Paul, *Stanislavski Method: Magic If and Illusion of the First Time*, 2013, http://broadwayeducators.com/stanislavski-method-magic-if-and-illusion-of-the-first-time/

29. Page 75
Adler, Arthur, *The Individual Psychology of Alfred Adler: A Systematic Presentation in Selections from his Writings*, H.L. Ansbacher & R.R Ansbacher, (Eds.), 1964, New York, NY: Harper Torchbooks, First Printed, 1956.

30. Page 78
Techtronic, Kamosi, Manuela and de Quincey, Thomas, *Pump up the Jam*, de Quincey 1989.
Author note: This is a song I will gladly sing *and* dance to when working with clients to get my point across about the power of expressiveness and being cognizant of the energy level you bring to a room.

31. Page 81
Shakespeare, William, *Hamlet*, Act I, scene iii, Hamlet.

32. Page 83

Peale, Norman Vincent, *The Power of Positive Thinking*, Prentice Hall, 1952.

Author note: I am going to confess here that I have never read any of Norman Vincet Peale's work, but I know many clients who have and have felt the work was life changing.

33. Page 83

(Playwright) Lynn, Kirk, *Lust Supper, (Director)* Richardson, Sarah, Rude Mechs, 1997.

Author note: Here's my ode to the Rude Mechs—and their founding members: Kathryn Blackbird, Madge Darlington, Kirsten Kern, Lana Lesley, Kirk Lynn, Sarah Richardson and Shawn Sides. They are a powerhouse of devised theatre-makers, playwrights, directors, movers, shakers and life altering artists based in Austin, Texas. I owe y'all buckets of gratitude for taking me on as an associate artist back in the day. I take your rude spirits with me in all I do.

34. Page 84

Mantra, *Om Namah Shivaya*,

https://www.sanskritmantra.com/article_info.php?articles_id=some-simple-mantras-for-those-just-starting-out-a-32

35. Page 85

Shakespeare, William, *Hamlet*, Act I, scene iii, Polonius.

36. Page 86

Lao-Tze,

https://hac.bard.edu/amor-mundi/lao-tze-on-how-thoughts-translate-int
o-destiny-2015-07-14

Author note: Some spell the name Lao Tzu or Laozi. This wasn't his
actual name, it's a title he was given to honor him as a teacher. He is
credited as being the 6th Century BC Chinese philosopher, and
contemporary of Confusius who began the teaching of Taoism. If you
want a quick hit on Taoism, I highly suggest the books *The Tao of Pooh*
and *Te of Piglet*, by Benjamin Hoff. Both of which combine the easy,
bumbling brilliance of Winnie the Pooh (and his sidekick Piglet) with
ancient wisdom of Lao-Tze.

Watch your thoughts; they become words.

Watch your words; they become actions.

Watch your actions; they become habits.

Watch your habits; they become character.

Watch your character; it becomes your destiny.

CPSIA information can be obtained
at www.ICGtesting.com
Printed in the USA
JSHW020807050623
42723JS00001B/97